A Small Book of

Kick-Arse Poetry

A Small Book of Kick-Arse Poetry

Dr. Lissa E. Judd

This book is written for 12 to 15 year olds who hate reading.

Don't worry if you normally get stuck on words - poetry is like music, and it will carry you past the mutter fumble bits.

You don't have to start at the beginning, and finish at the end. You can begin with a poem in the middle, if you want.

Don't show it to your parents, because they'll want it (either that, or they'll disapprove of the bad language).

Thanks to my son, Alam, for allowing me into his world.   L.E.J.

The Idea Factory
A division of I.C.E.P.S. Ltd.,
Wellington, New Zealand.

Copyright © 2012 by Lissa Elaine Judd

All rights reserved. This book or any portion thereof may not be reproduced or used in any manner whatsoever without the express written permission of the publisher except for the use of brief quotations in a book review.

International edition
Printed in the United States of America

First Printing, 2012

ISBN 978-0-473-22562-9

The Idea Factory
P.O. Box 57021 Mana
Porirua 5247
NEW ZEALAND
sales@anwyl.com

Contents

Grandma Ormond	6
Fiddlesticks	9
George	9
Dreams	10
Words	11
Eating my greens	12
My day	13
School	14
Summer afternoon	15
My dog	16
Clean my room?	17
The week before christmas	18
Little brother	19
Sunday	20
Oh God, I've wet the bed again	21
Bird bath	23
The monster	24
Man is smart	27
A nocturnal life	29
Questions	31
Christmas	32
Perfect little girls	35
Sport	36
My dog George	38
Loneliness	39
Mum's not very bright	40
Mathematics	42
I've got my own band	43
The brain	44
Wotherspoon	45
Looking after my things	47
ADHD	50
Swimming	52
It's so unfair	53
Lunchtime	54
Rain	55
The beach	57
The alligator	58

Grandma Ormrod

Granny Ormrod bought a duck.
She called him Mr Toot.
She bought a shotgun just for luck,
and taught him how to shoot.

He learned to ride a bicycle
and how to make a salad.
He learned to play the banjo
and how to sing a ballad.

He'd ride off to the local shops
to buy some bread and cheese.
"Good morning Mr Toot" they'd say,
"that'll be three dollars please."

He'd rifle through his feathers
and come up with the loot.
He'd place it on the countertop.
"Thank you Mr Toot."

One day when he went shopping
he spied a special treat:
brown bread with lovely seeds and grains -
Oh what a joy to eat!

It cost a little extra,
but he'd saved his pocket money.
He thought of Gran and how she'd smile
when eating it with honey.

He cycled up the driveway,
puffing in the heat,
but Grandma Ormrod wore a frown,
and slapped him on the beak.

"You didn't mop the floors" she said,
"before you went out shopping!"
"You lazy useless goddamn duck.."
and then, without stopping...

"What sort of bread is this?" she whined
"Its brown with seeds and grains!
I wanted white, you silly duck,
I think you have no brains"

"You get back on your bicycle
and cycle back to town,
and ask the man for fresh sliced white,
and don't come home with brown!"

So weary Mr Toot rode off,
his ducky legs were aching.
He held the bread bag with his beak;
his little heart was breaking.

The man exchanged his lovely bread,
with all the seeds and grains,
for one small loaf of fresh sliced white,
and he set off home again.

He cycled up the driveway,
puffing in the heat;
his heavy heart was pounding,
and he'd blisters on his feet.

"I've got the fresh sliced white" said Toot,
exhausted from his ride.
"You dreadful duck!" said thankless Gran,
"you're trekking mud inside!"

Mr Toot stood resolute,
the bread bag in his beak.
He pulled the trigger only once.
Gran Ormrod didn't speak.

Fiddlesticks

There are no pictures here except the ones inside your head.

Let the words become fat and slow,
All slather-gibber and milky-green,
languid and woozelling over the warm basalt.
Slithering, rolling, faster, sliding, falling
ploppetty plump into the tickley gruffley fiddlesticks.

George

Paws barely touch the ground,
fast as sound, George races towards the pond.
Digging quickly, grasses thickly
cover mouse-made burrows.
Tail wagging stiffly,
nose is sniffly sniffing,
urgent digging, snuffling
mice are scuffling
quick as light
with George in flight across the pasture.
Rodent running, doggy cunning,
hide in flaxes, heart pounding,
dog bounding, twisting, turning, waiting.
Mouse hating
game of chasing, cheating, eating.

Dreams

With my paintbox I can paint my dreams
in orange, blues, and greens,
and happy yellow in all these scenes
of winning everything it seems.
First in races, first at swimming,
first at sums, I'm good at winning
anything at all,
from spelling bees, to bandy knees,
and farting competitions,
where my emissions far exceeded my competitors'
in smell and sound, and hanging around,
and indeed so foul were they that Witherspoon
fainted sheer away,
and nurses slapped his cheeks and gave him air,
his Mum waiting anxiously near.
In my dreams I'm tall as heroes,
strong and clever, don't get zeroes
in my long division test,
its all easy,
days are long, the wind is breezy,
friends are true, and they don't tease me
anymore, 'coz I can do stuff they admire,
like wiggle my ears, and I aspire
to roll my tongue,
and with practice I'll get it done,
and then I'll be a champion,
in my dreams, at any rate, it seems.

Words

words sound
round or
thin and mean
or long and lean
but what do they mean?
how to choose
which one to use?
who blew blue clouds across
the pink sky?
why cry silver tears?
no one hears them falling
secretly at night
into the bend of your elbow

Eating my greens

Mum, if I eat all my tea,
including all my broccoli,
will I grow big enough
to stop that Jimmy Baraclough
from picking on me after school
and making me look like a fool?

Will scoffing all my peas
do anything to apease
that bully Barnes
and his friends in arms
who spill my drink and steal my lunch?
They are a very nasty bunch.

I'll gladly eat up all my greens
if you can guarantee that means
that no more kids will pick on me
or torment with bribery
or steal my stuff
I've had enough.

My day

boys swimming
faces grinning
water splashing
feet kicking
bubbles tickling
hair dripping
goggles fogging
girls giggling
fun having

mum baking
dad mowing
dogs barking
boys larking
birds singing
sun shining
bike riding
ground hitting
knee's bleeding
mum soothing
dad fixing

pizza eating
TV watching
teeth brushing
voices hushing
story reading
mum kissing
dog licking
teddy hugging
bed snuggling
happy sleeping

School

My teacher asks a lot of me,
he thinks that I am lazy.
He doesn't actually say as much
but I know he's not crazy
about my spelling or my writing,
or my lack of punctuation,
and I sometimes leave out little words
to add to his frustration.

But in that place inside my head where I keep my ideas
my words are all in order
and my thoughts are crystal clear.
The words get in a tangle as they travel down my arm,
and they spill out of my pencil all a fuddle muddle,
darn
I'll never get the hang of this.
The words don't look quite right.
What happened to the comma's? they've faded out of sight.
Did a punctuation monster grab the full stops on their way
to the page that I am writing on?
I hope that they're okay.

Summer afternoon

afternoon sun pressing hot
rocks baking shimmering
toetoes still
bare feet
quick quick dont stop until the grass
strawberries plucked fat and warm
secret shade
breath of breeze
lavender bees
sweet feast

My dog

my dog
sleek and bendy like a cat
the color of moonshadow.
tall as a foal
still as a crocodile

my dog
fast as sound
quiet as light
if you touch his supper dish
food gone in a blink

my dog
holds up his paw
washes your face with kisses
loyal as a swan
silly as a chook.

Clean my room?

You say I have to clean my room?
But Mum, my room's already clean -
the cleanest that it's ever been.
I cannot see
what needs to be
removed from this vicinity.
I cannot fathom what you mean.

You say I need to tidy up? -
to put my clothes and shoes away,
to gather up the vast array
of crispy socks,
and special rocks,
the comics, pens, and empty box?
You'd like to see the floor today?

I like my sheets a smudgy grey
with inky spots and stains galore.
I've laboured over this decor.
I've racing cars,
and bugs in jars,
and some half-eaten chocolate bars
under the pillow with quite a lot more.

The pizza underneath the bed
is part of my biology
assignment in ecology,
and if I store
my things in drawers
I'll never find them any more.
You owe me an apology.

The week before Christmas

'Twas the week before Christmas, and quiet as a mouse
little Billy Stinker crept through the house.
Looking in cupboards, looking in drawers,
looking under beds, looking behind doors.
Where were the presents? Where were they hidden?
He searched high and low and in places forbidden.

He needed to find them and check their dimensions.
He needed to work out his parents' intentions.
He needed to shake and to poke and to peer
to try and determine what gift was in there.
Could he see through the wrapping, or undo the string?
Could he palpate the contents or peek at the thing?

But then when he found it under the stairs
it hadn't been wrapped and he burst into tears.
It was just what he wanted - he couldn't believe his eyes.
He'd found his present - but lost his surprise.

Little brother

Little Willie with his mother
went to look for little brother.
They had left him at the beach
munching on a juicy peach.

Mum was wise and as he sat
she put on sunscreen and a hat
to stop him burning in the sun.
She said: "We're off, now you have fun!"

He waved goodbye, a peachy grin.
They both grinned peachily back at him.
They'd left him there an hour or two -
they both had other things to do.

He's nearly four, he cannot swim,
but Mum had mimed some strokes for him.
She showed him how to float and kick,
she's very wise - doesn't miss a trick.

So, where's the little rotter now?
He's wandered out of sight somehow.
He's left his peach stone on the sand.
Willie held his mother's hand.

Sunday

wispy rushes
breezy hushes
fishy swishy
icy splashy
girly giggly
goosey bumpy
sunny happy
camera snappy
doggy waggy
woofy crazy
summer lazy
oily drizzling
sausage sizzling
hungry smokey
fizzy drinking
bubbles tickling
daisy chain
home again

Oh God I've wet the bed again

Oh God I've wet the bed again.
My Mum says that's OK.
She says that I'll grow out of it.
Evidently, not today.

I'll hide my wet pyjamas
in the closet or the drawer,
and pull the duvet cover up,
just like I've done before,

so the dreadful deed is secret
'til the sun warms up the room
then the place gets awful stinky
as my linen starts to fume.

If I spend the night at friends'
I have pull-ups which I wear
hidden underneath my 'jamas,
but still I live in fear

that someone will discover these,
or there'll still be a leekage
and I lie awake in terror
of that smelly yellow seepage.

I've tried all sorts of fixes
from not drinking stuff at night,
and hormones that go up your nose,
and still I have my plight.

The buzzer thing in your underpants
that goes off loud when moist,
wakes everyone else in the household up
but I sleep through its noise.

I've thought of corks, or rubber bands
tied tight around my willy.
Mum says that it might drop off
and not to be so silly.

But God I wish that I'd wake up
when next I need to pee.
I'm sick of the embarassment
of wee all over me.

Bird bath

Mr Thrush, shy, drab,
not sure he wants to be seen in his bathing suit.
Tip toe stop. Look, listen.
Anyone watching?
A step
another
a little run,
stop, look. Listen.
He reaches the pond.
Look.
Listen, shhhh, careful,
but then he's in, splashing about gaily
like a jolly man in a tub
water under the arms
slop slosh slop slosh
head under
splash splish splash splish
shake shimmy
quick quick run away under a bush.

Mr Tui, bold, handsome,
poses on a nearby branch.
Casual glance over the shoulder,
a dandy on the diving board.
Splish
shake and out
back onto the diving board, pose, preen,
black emerald satin gleaming in the sunlight
splish
shake and out
fly away
kiss my ass, Thrush.

The monster

The monster underneath my bed
arrived three months ago, in May.
He said that it was cold outside
and asked if he could stay.
He told me he would help with chores
and tidy up my chest of drawers.
He said he almost never snores,
and he wouldn't be in the way.

He stood there trembling with the cold
his toes were turning blue.
He sneezed and wheezed and spluttered.
What else could I do?
I said that he could stay a week,
he'd have to wash his smelly feet,
and would he like a cake to eat?
He said that he'd like two!

I got him warm pyjamas
and woollen socks to wear,
a knitted hat and fleecy gloves-
he looked a little queer.
I said that he would have to keep
his promise not to snore, or creep
about the house instead of sleep,
in case my Mum should hear.

I went to get some cakes for him,
and chose two of the best.
He ate them both then ran downstairs
and gobbled all the rest!
And then he ate tomorrow's lunch
and polished off the ginger crunch.
Well, I dont know, I have a hunch
he's going to be a pest.

I grabbed the monster by the arm
and marched him back upstairs
and tucked him up beneath my bed
and made him say his prayers.
He fell asleep but I slept light,
I heard some thumping in the night -
I grabbed my torch, turned on the light
to catch him unawares.

And there, illuminated by my torch,
the monster stood with brush in hand;
he'd painted murals on my walls -
he thought that they looked rather grand.
One wall was now a rural scene,
another was a wolverine,
and one - a portrait of the Queen.
Its not as I had planned.

I tucked him up in bed once more,
and pondered how I might explain
the monstrous artwork to my Mum.
She'll think I've gone insane.
I lay awake with heavy heart,
tormented by the monster's art,
this was an inauspicious start.
He's snoring like a train.

When the morning light comes in
I survey all the damage wraught.
I can't see my school uniform -
the new one mother bought.
And then I spy some monster poo,
a little pile of greenish goo,
with little bits of navy blue -
I can't wear that, I thought.

And this is how it's been since he
arrived three months ago in May.
He wrecks my things and drives me mad;
he's always in the way.
But every day he makes me smile.
We've been best friends now for a while.
You cannot help but like his style.
I hope that he will stay.

Man is smart

Man is smart,
he's got the goods.
He invented fire,
he burned down woods

to graze his cows,
or goats, or sheep,
or build a carpark
for his jeep.

He drills for oil
to fuel this beast
which carries him
to town to feast

upon the fries
and fatty fare;
he's way too fat
to walk to there.

His house is huge,
his lawn is small,
he can't afford
to furnish it all.

He visits nature
once a year;
he takes his jeep,
and a crate of beer.

The tiger and
the bear can stay
in a little bit
of land away

from houses and
from flocks of sheep,
as they're not there
for the bears to eat.

And if they wander
in to prey,
he'll shoot the varmints
anyway.

Oh darn! They've gone!
Oh, never mind!
There's other species
left behind

for Man to look at
once a year,
when he takes his jeep,
and a crate of beer.

A nocturnal life

I'd like to list the things I've done
but cannot think of many -
I'm actually having trouble
trying to make a list of any.

I've watched TV, I've watched TV,
I've watched TV some more.
I've also played computer games.
How many's that? That's four.

Hang on a minute, that's not right,
it's actually only two.
There must be something more to life -
some other thing I do.

The X-box and the i-pad
and the other sorts of screens
are where I choose to spend my life,
vicariously, it seems.

I sleep all day, I'm up all night,
in darkness like a bat.
My parents think it quite bizarre
that I should live like that.

But here I have control of life,
my virtual reality.
I stroke, or key, or toggle bits -
its isn't just banality.

I feel secure, I am in charge -
my characters don't tease;
they do not mock or bully me;
I win these games with ease.

But one day soon when I feel safe
I'll step out in the light.
My parents wont remember me -
I'll give them both a fright!

Questions

What is armpit hair there for?
Can anybody tell me more?
For boys it may be all the rage -
it tells they've reached a certain age,
but girls don't want the stuff to grow.
Why is there, I'd like to know?

When do you think that I'll be glad
of the algebra lessons that I've had?
Will they help me in my mission
to be a dentist or beautician?
When will all this have a use -
this mathematics so obtuse?

How come mothers are so wise,
they always catch you telling lies?
How do they know it's all BS -
those fibs you craft with such finesse?
You make it so believable,
how come its inconceivable?

Why do holidays go so fast?
No matter how long, they never last.
Christmas is over a year away!
Who stretched out the length of the day?
Time lasts longer when at school.
Who was it that made this rule?

Christmas

Aunty Mary's in the sherry,
giving Dad advice.
She said if he'd apply himself
we could live somewhere nice.

She thought our house was very small,
the neighbourhood was seedy;
perhaps he'd like to work for Tom,
then we'd not be so needy.

Aunty grabbed a Christmas pie,
and said that Tom was big
in property and some such stuff.
She paused to take a swig.

"Where did you get the ham?" she asked
"I'd not go there again!
The vegetables were overcooked,
the pudding: rather plain."

"We'd have you all at our place
for a decent Christmas spread,
but we don't like to be show-offs,
so we'll slum it here instead."

"I'd help you with the washing up,
but I'd be in the way.
I'll have another glass of your
cheap sherry if I may."

Through all of this my Uncle Tom
sat snoring in his chair,
his chest adorned with cakey crumbs,
his breath perfumed with beer.

Grandma said our gift to her
looked just the same, she's sure,
as what she gave to us last year,
or perhaps the year before?

She'd hidden in her pocket
chocolate almonds and some fudge.
She tried to shoo the dog away,
but Iggy wouldn't budge.

Sniffing at the chocolate,
Iggy followed Gran around,
his nose glued firmly to her hip -
a most determined hound!

My little sister, turning green,
complained of stomach ache.
She'd eaten lots of chocolates,
and too much Christmas cake.

She threw up on the carpet -
some smelly Christmas goo,
and cousin Ollie stood in it,
which made him throw up too.

My sister felt much better;
poor Ollie - he looked pale.
The dog cleaned all the mess up,
propelled by wagging tail.

Oh what a jolly Christmas!
Its like this every year.
Its good that we can celebrate
the birth of - who was it?
Oh, I dunno.
Have another piece of cake.

Perfect little girls

Perfect little girls are we -
so polite to family,
pretty clothes and shining hair,
sparkly earrings in our ears,
rosy cheeks and polished nails,
pouty lips and ponytails.
We're admired by all the school,
but if you cross us, you're a fool -
we're the cyber-bully-bitches,
just a bunch of pretty witches -
you'll have no friends any more,
when we commence our texting war.
We're united, you're alone;
our weapon is the mobile phone.
We are charming, well regarded,
everyone thinks you're retarded.
Perfect little girls are we.
You're a loser - dont you see?

Usually if you wait a while
those fake-nice girls with practiced smile,
whose outer charm's a thin veneer,
their moral cupboard lying bare -
usually life will come up trumps:
they're on a road with lots of bumps.
It may be years 'til they receive
delicious payback for their deeds.
When they're hit with life's thunderclouds -
will you forgive, or lol?

Sport

I hate sport and it hates me,
my legs just won't go fast.
I cannot do gymnastics,
and in races I come last.

No one wants me on their team -
I cannot catch the ball.
I try to make a grab for it,
but usually trip and fall.

Recklessly I swing my bat,
determined to succeed;
why does the pitcher throw the thing
with such ferocious speed?

In tennis if I hit the ball
it goes way in the air,
and lands a mile away in scrub -
it really isn't fair.

In the pool I go like mad
and kick and splash and bubble,
while others glide past silently -
for them it is no trouble.

The kids at school poke fun at me
because I'm fat and spotty.
This body I've been issued with
is really rather grotty.

They say that sport is good for you -
it keeps you lean and fit;
you learn important values,
and all that sort of shit.

It really just defeats me,
and I've learned that folk are mean.
I think I've hurt my ankle,
and I wish that I were clean.

If only sumo wrestling
was available at school -
I reckon its the only sport
where I'd not look a fool.

I smile as I imagine
the pleading in their eyes,
as I squash all those smug bastards
between my ample thighs.

My dog George.

My dog George is my best pal -
he doesn't say much, but he listens well;
he's always cheerful, never sad -
he's the best friend I ever had.

He comes when called, he chases sticks,
he gives you lots of kissy licks.
He wags his tail, holds up his paw;
he sleeps beside me, on the floor.

Even when I come home late,
he's always waiting by the gate.
He's buried all my teddy bears,
but gosh we've had fun all these years.

He used to race around like crazy,
but now he's getting old and lazy,
even though he's in his teens -
for dogs that's different, so it seems.

Poor old George is growing lumps,
and he's losing his grey hair in clumps.
His breath is now a toxic fume,
his farts will richly fill the room.

But then this morning George was weird -
I got my Mum 'cos I was scared.
He's fast asleep and he won't wake,
no matter how I prod or shake.

His breathing stops for ages then
its fast and deep, and stops again.
He seems so strangely still and calm,
and yet I'm filled with such alarm.

Mum says George has gone away,
he's walking up to Heaven today.
When his journey has succeeded
this old body won't be needed.

I waited there with my best friend;
I held his paw until the end.
We buried him beneath a tree;
his memory's safe inside of me.

Loneliness

You think that you are on your own,
but trust me, it's not true -
there's lots of little creatures
that you cart around with you.

Your bowel is full of microbes,
little mites live down your hairs,
there's lots of creepy-crawlies
of which you're unawares.

So next time when you're lonely,
and feel a little blue -
think of all these little friends
accompanying you.

Mum's not very bright

I love my Mum, don't get me wrong,
but she's not very bright.
I try hard to explain to her...
you could go on all night.
There's so much that she doesn't get,
its obvious to me, and yet
she seems determined to forget,
and then to think she's right!

Oh, imagine the ignominy
of turning up to school
in a waterproof red jacket -
God - you'd look a fool!
I tried my hardest to explain,
that even in torrential rain
I won't wear that damn thing again -
it simply isnt cool!

She packs a wholesome, healthy lunch
into my bag each day.
There's sandwiches and fruit and stuff:
I chuck it all away.
My friends, they all buy chips and pies;
I wish I had some salty fries.
Why is my mother so damn wise?
Why don't I have a say?

It's SO exasperating that I'm
meant to do some chores -
just give me my allowance!
I deserve it because:
I go to school instead of play,
I live with you lot every day,
there really isn't any way
I'm vacuuming the floors!

I need more pocket money, as I've
lots of things to buy,
but Mum says that I've got enough
and doesn't even try
to understand my fiscal aims
to get a lot more X-box games,
and clothes that have designer names:
just basic supplies!

Despite my mother's sluggish wit,
I grudgingly agree
her chocolate muffins are the best;
she cleans my clothes for free.
She makes me laugh, we have some fun;
I love her more than anyone.
When everything else is said and done,
she wants the best for me.

Mathematics

If it takes two men six days to build a bridge,
how many eggs can a cow lay, in a week?

Four.

What if the men worked longer hours?
Is it a brown cow, or black and white?

It's still four.

Mr Snodgrass says it's logical.
He says it will enrich our lives.

How long a lunchbreak do the men get?
Mr Snodgrass says don't be smart.

But I'm not smart.
If I was smart, I'd know why it was four.

I've drawn a nice picture of a cow.
That has to count for something.

I've got my own band

hip hop
bee bop
d' doo wop
b' bee bop
d' diddly doo
d' dee wop
bee barp
barp barp
d' doo wop
bee bop
d' diddly wop
b' bee bop
d' diddly doo
d' dee wop
ch ch
ch ch
ch chittity ump
ch chittity ump
barp barp
ch chittity ump
ch chittity ump
barp barp
d' diddly doo
ch ch
ch chittity ump
d' diddly doo
ch chittity ump
d' diddly doo
b' bee bop
d' doo wop
bee barp
d' doodly dah
dump dum
d' dum
p' BOOM

The brain

Your brain is where you keep your thoughts -
it's found inside your head;
it's like a sort of greyish cheese,
but walnut-shaped instead.

Your skull is thick to keep it safe,
and stop it getting bruised.
My brain is just as good as new -
its hardly ever used.

I wonder how come memories
don't all leak out your nose -
that snot might be arithmetic
escaping, I suppose.

Hold your breath and listen hard,
your eyes closed really tight -
you'll sometimes hear a whooshy noise
inside your head at night.

Is that the brain's machinery
assembling your ideas,
concocting all your fantasies,
and bottling all your fears?

Who do you think's in charge of it?
Surely it's not me!
It functions independently,
as far as I can see.

Wotherspoon

Billy Wotherspoon was sick,
he stayed at home today;
his tummy felt a little ick -
he didn't go and play.

His Mum prepared a chicken soup
and gave him lots to drink -
it only made him want to poop,
and throw up in the sink.

On the toilet Billy stayed
and listened to the sound
his model railway engine made
as it went chuffing 'round.

It circled underneath the loo
and out the other side;
it tooted as he did a poo -
he watched his train with pride.

Billy's Mum says that he's got
a gastroenteritis.
He should've washed his hands a lot
'cos then the germs don't like us.

"Wash your hands" his mother said
"and come and drink this up".
She tucked him back into his bed,
and handed him a cup.

Billy lay there queezily,
a virus in his tum;
sleep did not come easily -
he felt a little glum.

As he dozed erratically,
Billy made a vow:
to wash his hands fanatically.
He's got diarrhea now.

Looking after my things

If you give your mobile phone
a soaking in the rain,
I think you'll find (as I have done)
that it won't go again.

The trouble is, I didn't learn,
I've soaked another three;
I've lost one on the way to school,
and dropped one from a tree.

If you're on your skateboard
and you fall down on your bum -
you've smashed another mobile phone
(best not tell your Mum).

The jersey that we wear at school
looks manky when it's new -
I cut some holes into the cuffs,
to let my thumbs poke through.

I lost one jersey on the train,
another on the bus;
my Dad has bought a third one
but he's making quite a fuss.

He says I should appreciate
the cost of all this stuff,
and next time I can buy my own -
he's really had enough.

My X-box overheated
and it wont go anymore:
the red ring of doom again -
it's happened twice before.

I can't use my computer
'cos there's malware on my disc.
I turned the anti-virus off -
it was a silly risk,

especially as I like to
download everything that's free:
that virus-laden software
from the pirate company.

I like to work out how things go
by taking them apart.
It's tricky reassembling them -
at least I make a start.

There's usually bits left over
and I keep them in my drawer -
they'll come in very useful
for something else, I'm sure.

I took apart my radio,
and now its working swell;
I've hidden the remote control -
it didn't fare so well.

The clock is going nicely
its cogs investigated;
the TV I dismantled
is now discombobulated.

I think that when I grow up
I will be an engineer;
my parents sigh and roll their eyes,
resignedly, I fear.

ADHD

Stinky Jones was hyperactive -
couldn't keep him still;
he was a whole lot better
on the days he took his pill.

He couldn't concentrate at school -
it bristled with distractions;
there was no time to think ahead
to stop impulse reactions.

He tried so hard to understand
the words his teacher said -
but they were drowned out by the roar
of static in his head.

His classmates knuckle down and work
but Stinky plays the fool;
the lesson's quite opaque to him -
he's miserable at school.

He gets up at the crack of dawn
and goes to bed quite late;
his inner clock is stuck on 'now' -
he really cannot wait.

Stinky chatters on all day
he's barely time to eat;
at school he wanders 'round the class -
he won't stay in his seat.

Reading is impossible -
the letters will not stay:
they move and turn and twist in such a
dizzy queezy way.

Numbers also baffle him:
he cannot work it out-
how to turn those symbols
into actual amounts.

Concepts like before and after,
nearly, soon, and yet -
are all such vague abstractions
that he really doesn't get.

It's all so darn frustrating
and he's suddenly enraged -
he's punched a hole into the wall
before his brain engaged.

His Mum says that he's got to make
the best of what he's got:
utilise his strengths to make
his life a better lot.

So Stinky takes his pills on days
he needs to keep a grip
on his mental perturbations,
but on weekends he lets rip.

The rest of us perceive the world
in sequence and in bits,
but Stinky sees the whole of things:
an enigmatic wit.

He answers questions no one asks -
he thinks a different way;
he has a most extraordinary gift-
he'll realise it one day.

Swimming

How come rats and elephants
can both swim really well?
Neither have had lessons,
as far as I can tell.

They don't do any practice
to hone their swimming styles -
but dump them in the ocean
and they both can swim for miles.

It's so unfair

Mum says that my skirt's too short,
my neckline is too tarty;
she says that I can't spend the night
at my friend Emma's party.

She won't let me drink alcohol;
she treats me like a child.
For heavens sake! I'm now thirteen! -
it's not like I've gone wild!

I don't see what the problem is
with piercings in my brow,
and tongue, and ears, and lower lip.
Boy, is she a cow!

The words I've tattooed on my breast
are really all the rage.
Mum says they'll look ludicrous
when I am middle aged.

I hate all these restrictions-
it's really SO unfair;
I'm going to sulk an hour or two,
and then I'll dye my hair.

Lunchtime

names called
punch thrown
nose bleed
shirt torn
much scorn
fight back
strength lack
too thin
must win
swift kick
arm block
head lock
egged on
don't cry
must try
fists fly
lunch time
bell rings
last swings
last cuss
no fuss
walk away
another day
he'll pay

Rain

Water running in my eyes,
dripping off my nose;
it's gone all squelchy in my shoes-
I'm splashing with my toes.
My hands are blue,
my cheeks are too,
I've ten more minutes walk to do;
I'm soaked right through my clothes.

Mum will say it's all my fault -
I knew that it would pour -
I should have packed that waterproof
red jacket I abhore.
I'd rather get
supremely wet -
I've not worn that red jacket yet.
Hell will freeze before.

I slop into the kitchen
leaving puddles in my wake:
little ponds of water,
with every step I take.
Its warm in here,
I shed my gear,
I put on something dry to wear,
and have a piece of cake.

I'm sitting by the fireplace,
basking in the heat -
I'm only inches from the flames,
roasting hands and feet.
My cheeks are red,
I've jam and bread,
the steam is rising from my head.
I need some more to eat.

I've left a pile of soggy clothes
lying in a heap.
My schoolbag has a lake in it -
my mother wants to weep.
My phone won't go,
and that's a blow,
and then my mother wants to know
which sodden books to keep.

She tips the water from my bag,
she pours it from my shoes,
she puts them both before the fire.
I don't think she's amused.
"Next time don't
forget your coat
and then your things won't be afloat"
(an angry tone was used).

But next time that it's pouring
on my way home from the train,
you can guarantee that I will
get a soaking once again.
It isn't cool
to look a fool,
and wear a raincoat home from school -
I'd rather wear the rain.

The beach*

sunshine
sublime
seaside
high tide
salt spray
all day
starfish
seaweed
I need
sunscreen
ice-cream
hot sand
icy dip
tidal rip
swept away
bad day
out to sea
goodness me

* dedicated to Harry Sparkle

The alligator

Peter's got an alligator
living in the bath;
it ate his little brother -
it only left his scarf.

He bought it into school one day,
to show us all his pet -
although it's eight feet long it hasn't
finished growing yet.

Peter made his alligator
sit down on a chair;
he said its name was Phillip and:
"you'll hardly know he's here".

Mrs Murphy wasn't sure,
she thought there was a rule -
she didn't think that alligators
were allowed in school.

"Phillip", Mrs Murphy said,
"should be securely tied
to the post outside the bike-shed;
he shouldn't come inside."

But", protested Peter,
"he'd get awfully cold out there".
Mrs Murphy said: "He should
have brought a coat to wear."

Peter left his alligator
parked outside the shed.
"You stay here until I'm back
at 3 o'clock" he said.

But Peter got detention
and was kept in class 'til four -
his only thought was Phillip
as he bolted out the door.

"Oh God, I'm late!" moaned Peter
as he raced towards the shed.
"Poor Phillip, he'll be cold, and he'll
be wanting to be fed".

He noticed in the distance
all the bicycles still there -
"They must have all walked home today"
he said as he drew near.

And if that wasn't odd enough
(and Peter now looked troubled),
in his absence Phillip's girth
had very nearly doubled.

Phillip gave a reptile burp -
it had a boyish smell,
and several scarves were found nearby:
"This does not bode well."

Peter picked up all the scarves-
he put them with the others:
some from children down the street;
the blue one was his brother's.

A lesson can be learned from this:
(you really musn't laugh)
if you own an alligator,
do not wear a scarf.

www.ingramcontent.com/pod-product-compliance
Lightning Source LLC
Chambersburg PA
CBHW061251040426
42444CB00010B/2348